POV: My Family Got Bigger (and Louder)

Pumpkin's Version

PUMPKIN'S DIARY

By Callie Cruse

For freebies and extra's please scan here

The Blended Diaries Series

Begin Again Books

theblendeddiaries.com

Dear Reader,

Welcome to The Blended Diaries, a collection of stories about families that don't always match but somehow still fit.
This one is told by Pumpkin, the small scruffy dog who didn't exactly ask for a blended family but ended up in one anyway.
He's here to sniff out the truth, nap through the chaos, and prove that love can be messy and still pretty great.

Woofs and wishes,
Callie x

Reviewing this book takes 2 minutes and earns you a tail wag from Pumpkin

Published by Begin Again Books
Printed in the country where this book was purchased.
For more, visit theblendeddiaries.com

PUMPKIN

That is me.
Small and scruffy.

NINA

One of my mums.
Rory and Maggie
are her children.

RORY

Makes loud noises.
Drops food.
I love this about him.

MAGGIE

Loves glitter.
Loves giving belly rubs.

We lived together first.
Then we moved in with Libby, Taylor,
and Caleb and life got extra noisy.

LIBBY

My other mum.
Taylor and Caleb are
her children.

TAYLOR

Talks loud. Pretends she
doesn't like me (she does)

CALEB

Sings on the toilet.
Throws sticks for me.

Now we all live in one busy house.
Two families together.
One big family now

ENTRY ONE: MY NEW HOUSE

Hello.

I'm Pumpkin.

I'm a dog.

I used to live with Nina, Rory, and Maggie.

Now we live with more people.

It's louder.

It's messier.

There's not much space for naps.

But Rory still drops food.

And Maggie still gives belly rubs.

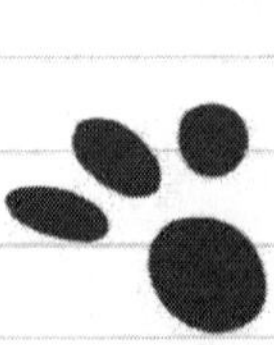

So maybe... it's not so bad.

Potato Chip

ENTRY TWO: NO SOFA FOR ME

At our old house, I had my spot on the sofa.

It was soft. And mine.

Now?

Too many bums.

No room for Pumpkin.

I tried to squeeze in.

Someone sat on my tail.

Now I sleep on my blanket on the floor.

It smells like wet dog.

Sigh.

OUCH!
PUMPKIN'S NEW SPOT

ENTRY THREE: TOO MANY FEET

This house has too many feet.

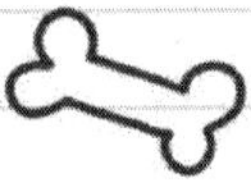

Big ones. Small ones.

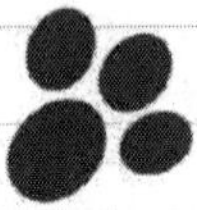

Fast, stompy ones.

They trip over me.

They step on my tail.

Even when I hide.

I miss when it was just me, Nina, Rory, and Maggie.

Less feet. More naps.

TOO
MANY
FEET

ENTRY FOUR: LOUD, LOUD, LOUD

Taylor talks loud.

Caleb sings on the toilet.

Rory roars like a lion.

Maggie shouts about glitter.

Even the telly is loud.

I hide under the table.

It's my quiet place.

SEND HELP

ENTRY FIVE: SNACK MISTAKE

Nina packed Rory a snack for school.

But... it was MY dog biscuit!

At lunch, Rory shouted,

"Eww! This is for dogs!"

Everyone laughed.

Rory didn't.

I didn't even get my biscuit back.

Very unfair.

EWW! THIS IS FOR DOGS
SCHOOL

ENTRY SIX: NO WALK TODAY

I sat by the door.

Tail wagging. Ready.

But no one said "Walkies."

They were too busy shouting.

So I waited.

And waited.

No walk.

Just noise.

Maybe tomorrow.

CALENDAR

ENTRY SEVEN: BIG BATH TROUBLE

Today, Nina said I smelt like bins.

That means one thing...

Bath time.

I ran behind the sofa.

They found me.

I tried under the table.

They found me again.

The bath was bubbly.

I got soap in my ear.

Rory called me "Wet Dog Wobblehead."

I didn't like it.

But after, Nina gave me a cuddle.

And a biscuit. 

So... maybe it wasn't all bad.

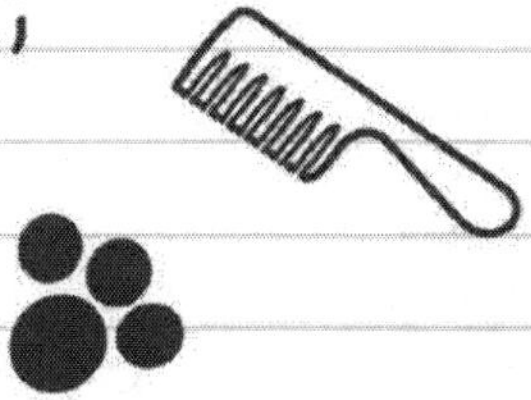

ENTRY EIGHT: THE BEST WALK EVER

Today, we all went on a walk.

A proper one! With leads and snacks!

Rory wore a cape.

Maggie brought a clipboard.

Taylor rolled her eyes the whole time.

Caleb had muddy socks. Again.

I sniffed every tree.

Nina held my lead.

Libby gave me a treat.

No one shouted.

No one cried.

It was perfect.

I wagged my tail all the way home.

ENTRY NINE: TWO MUMS

I have two mums.

Libby and Nina.

Some people say, "That's different."

But to me, it's just normal.

Libby gives belly rubs.

Nina sneaks me snacks.

They both love me.

And they love each other.

Two mums.

One family.

Lots of love.

YEP, I'VE GOT TWO MUMS.

ENTRY TEN: BLENDED FAMILY

My family is big now.

I used to live with three people.

Now there are seven (including me).

It's louder.

It's messier.

But it's fun.

Rory makes me giggle.

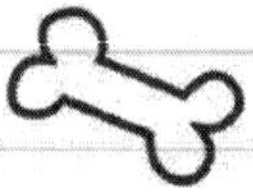

Maggie reads me stories.

Taylor lets me in her room (sometimes).

Caleb throws my ball.

It's not always easy.

But we're learning.

And I think...

I like it here sometimes.

ENTRY ELEVEN: THE LOUDEST POO

Today, Rory left the bathroom door open.

Again.

Then we all heard it.

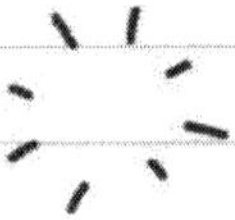

PLOP.

Splash.

"DON'T COME IN!" he yelled.

Taylor was almost sick..

Caleb laughed.

Even I ran off

and it smelled worse than my poos!

This place is never quiet.

Not even for poos.

DON'T COME IN!

ENTRY TWELVE: THE BISCUIT BATTLE

Maggie dropped a custard cream.

It bounced.

Rory saw it.

I saw it too.

We both ran.

He slid. I skidded.

The biscuit rolled under the table.

I got there first.

Victory!

Rory said, "That was mine!"

But floor biscuits belong to dogs.

ENTRY THIRTEEN: ALL TOGETHER

Today we all watched a film.

On one sofa.

Squished in like socks in a drawer.

Taylor rolled her eyes.

Caleb shared his popcorn.

Maggie put a blanket on me.

Rory laughed so hard, he snorted.

Libby and Nina smiled at each other.

No one argued.

Not even once.

It felt... nice.

Like we were all one big pack.

I am starting to feel like I do belong here.

ENTRY FOURTEEN: MY SPOT

Today I found a sunny patch on the carpet.

Just the right size for me.

Warm. Quiet. Perfect.

No feet stepped on me.

No toys flew past my head.

No one shouted.

It was just me and the sun.

Maggie walked past and said,

"That's Pumpkin's spot."

I think she's right.

It is my spot now.

THAT'S PUMPKIN'S SPOT.

ENTRY FIFTEEN: OUR FAMILY

This house is still noisy.

Still messy.

Still full.

But now, I know where my bowl is.

Where my blanket goes.

Where I belong.

Rory shares his snacks.

Maggie draws me with sparkles.

Taylor talks to me when no one's around.

Caleb threw a stick yesterday, just for me.

Libby gives the best chin rubs.

Nina sings to me while she makes toast.

And me?

I wag my tail.

We're not perfect.

But we're a family.

And I'm an important part of it.

DRAW YOUR FAMILY

Draw everyone in your family, including pets if you have them.

Don't forget yourself! Write one thing you like about each person.

MY FAVOURITE FAMILY DAY

Draw or write about your favourite day with your family.

What made it special and who made you laugh the most?

IF I WERE IN CHARGE FOR A DAY

If you were the boss of your family for one whole day, what rules would you make?
(Pumpkin says rule number one should be extra snacks.)

"Did you enjoy Pumpkin's Diary?
Scan here to tell Pumpkin what you thought!"

Find more fun family stuff at
www.TheBlendedDiaries.com

Made in the USA
Middletown, DE
07 December 2025

24340491R00024